I0462693

THE PERSONAL

INTERNET
PASSWORD

ORGANIZER

A

WEB NAME:

WEB ADDRESS:

USERNAME:

PASSWORD:

NOTES:

WEB NAME:

WEB ADDRESS:

USERNAME:

PASSWORD:

NOTES:

WEB NAME:

WEB ADDRESS:

USERNAME:

PASSWORD:

NOTES:

WEB NAME:

WEB ADDRESS:

A

USERNAME:

PASSWORD:

NOTES:

WEB NAME:

WEB ADDRESS:

USERNAME:

PASSWORD:

NOTES:

WEB NAME:

WEB ADDRESS:

USERNAME:

PASSWORD:

NOTES:

A

WEB NAME:

WEB ADDRESS:

USERNAME:

PASSWORD:

NOTES:

WEB NAME:

WEB ADDRESS:

USERNAME:

PASSWORD:

NOTES:

WEB NAME:

WEB ADDRESS:

USERNAME:

PASSWORD:

NOTES:

WEB NAME:

WEB ADDRESS:

A

USERNAME:

PASSWORD:

NOTES:

WEB NAME:

WEB ADDRESS:

USERNAME:

PASSWORD:

NOTES:

WEB NAME:

WEB ADDRESS:

USERNAME:

PASSWORD:

NOTES:

A

WEB NAME:

WEB ADDRESS:

USERNAME:

PASSWORD:

NOTES:

WEB NAME:

WEB ADDRESS:

USERNAME:

PASSWORD:

NOTES:

WEB NAME:

WEB ADDRESS:

USERNAME:

PASSWORD:

NOTES:

WEB NAME:

WEB ADDRESS:

A

USERNAME:

PASSWORD:

NOTES:

WEB NAME:

WEB ADDRESS:

USERNAME:

PASSWORD:

NOTES:

WEB NAME:

WEB ADDRESS:

USERNAME:

PASSWORD:

NOTES:

B

WEB NAME:

WEB ADDRESS:

USERNAME:

PASSWORD:

NOTES:

WEB NAME:

WEB ADDRESS:

USERNAME:

PASSWORD:

NOTES:

WEB NAME:

WEB ADDRESS:

USERNAME:

PASSWORD:

NOTES:

WEB NAME: _____

WEB ADDRESS: _____

USERNAME: _____ *B*

PASSWORD: _____

NOTES: _____

_____

_____

WEB NAME: _____

WEB ADDRESS: _____

USERNAME: _____

PASSWORD: _____

NOTES: _____

_____

_____

WEB NAME: _____

WEB ADDRESS: _____

USERNAME: _____

PASSWORD: _____

NOTES: _____

_____

_____

B

WEB NAME: _____

WEB ADDRESS: _____

USERNAME: _____

PASSWORD: _____

NOTES: _____

_____

_____

WEB NAME: _____

WEB ADDRESS: _____

USERNAME: _____

PASSWORD: _____

NOTES: _____

_____

_____

WEB NAME: _____

WEB ADDRESS: _____

USERNAME: _____

PASSWORD: _____

NOTES: _____

_____

_____

WEB NAME:

WEB ADDRESS:

USERNAME: *B*

PASSWORD:

NOTES:

WEB NAME:

WEB ADDRESS:

USERNAME:

PASSWORD:

NOTES:

WEB NAME:

WEB ADDRESS:

USERNAME:

PASSWORD:

NOTES:

B

WEB NAME: _____

WEB ADDRESS: _____

USERNAME: _____

PASSWORD: _____

NOTES: _____

_____

_____

WEB NAME: _____

WEB ADDRESS: _____

USERNAME: _____

PASSWORD: _____

NOTES: _____

_____

_____

WEB NAME: _____

WEB ADDRESS: _____

USERNAME: _____

PASSWORD: _____

NOTES: _____

_____

_____

WEB NAME: _____

WEB ADDRESS: _____

USERNAME: _____ *B*

PASSWORD: _____

NOTES: _____

_____

_____

WEB NAME: _____

WEB ADDRESS: _____

USERNAME: _____

PASSWORD: _____

NOTES: _____

_____

_____

WEB NAME: _____

WEB ADDRESS: _____

USERNAME: _____

PASSWORD: _____

NOTES: _____

_____

_____

WEB NAME: _____

WEB ADDRESS: _____

USERNAME: _____

e **PASSWORD:** _____

NOTES: _____

_____

_____

WEB NAME: _____

WEB ADDRESS: _____

USERNAME: _____

PASSWORD: _____

NOTES: _____

_____

_____

WEB NAME: _____

WEB ADDRESS: _____

USERNAME: _____

PASSWORD: _____

NOTES: _____

_____

_____

WEB NAME:

WEB ADDRESS:

USERNAME:

PASSWORD:

NOTES:

WEB NAME:

WEB ADDRESS:

USERNAME:

PASSWORD:

NOTES:

WEB NAME:

WEB ADDRESS:

USERNAME:

PASSWORD:

NOTES:

WEB NAME:

WEB ADDRESS:

USERNAME:

e **PASSWORD:**

NOTES:

WEB NAME:

WEB ADDRESS:

USERNAME:

PASSWORD:

NOTES:

WEB NAME:

WEB ADDRESS:

USERNAME:

PASSWORD:

NOTES:

WEB NAME:

WEB ADDRESS:

USERNAME:

PASSWORD:

NOTES:

WEB NAME:

WEB ADDRESS:

USERNAME:

PASSWORD:

NOTES:

WEB NAME:

WEB ADDRESS:

USERNAME:

PASSWORD:

NOTES:

WEB NAME:

WEB ADDRESS:

USERNAME:

e **PASSWORD:**

NOTES:

WEB NAME:

WEB ADDRESS:

USERNAME:

PASSWORD:

NOTES:

WEB NAME:

WEB ADDRESS:

USERNAME:

PASSWORD:

NOTES:

WEB NAME: _____

WEB ADDRESS: _____

USERNAME: _____

PASSWORD: _____

NOTES: _____

_____

_____

WEB NAME: _____

WEB ADDRESS: _____

USERNAME: _____

PASSWORD: _____

NOTES: _____

_____

_____

WEB NAME: _____

WEB ADDRESS: _____

USERNAME: _____

PASSWORD: _____

NOTES: _____

_____

_____

WEB NAME:

WEB ADDRESS:

USERNAME:

PASSWORD:

D **NOTES:**

WEB NAME:

WEB ADDRESS:

USERNAME:

PASSWORD:

NOTES:

WEB NAME:

WEB ADDRESS:

USERNAME:

PASSWORD:

NOTES:

WEB NAME:

WEB ADDRESS:

USERNAME:

PASSWORD:

NOTES:

WEB NAME:

WEB ADDRESS:

USERNAME:

PASSWORD:

NOTES:

WEB NAME:

WEB ADDRESS:

USERNAME:

PASSWORD:

NOTES:

D

WEB NAME: _____

WEB ADDRESS: _____

USERNAME: _____

PASSWORD: _____

NOTES: _____

_____

_____

WEB NAME: _____

WEB ADDRESS: _____

USERNAME: _____

PASSWORD: _____

NOTES: _____

_____

_____

WEB NAME: _____

WEB ADDRESS: _____

USERNAME: _____

PASSWORD: _____

NOTES: _____

_____

_____

WEB NAME:

WEB ADDRESS:

USERNAME:

PASSWORD:

NOTES:

D

WEB NAME:

WEB ADDRESS:

USERNAME:

PASSWORD:

NOTES:

WEB NAME:

WEB ADDRESS:

USERNAME:

PASSWORD:

NOTES:

WEB NAME:

WEB ADDRESS:

USERNAME:

PASSWORD:

D **NOTES:**

WEB NAME:

WEB ADDRESS:

USERNAME:

PASSWORD:

NOTES:

WEB NAME:

WEB ADDRESS:

USERNAME:

PASSWORD:

NOTES:

WEB NAME:

WEB ADDRESS:

USERNAME:

PASSWORD:

NOTES:

D

WEB NAME:

WEB ADDRESS:

USERNAME:

PASSWORD:

NOTES:

WEB NAME:

WEB ADDRESS:

USERNAME:

PASSWORD:

NOTES:

WEB NAME:

WEB ADDRESS:

USERNAME:

PASSWORD:

NOTES:

WEB NAME:

WEB ADDRESS:

USERNAME:

PASSWORD:

NOTES:

WEB NAME:

WEB ADDRESS:

USERNAME:

PASSWORD:

NOTES:

WEB NAME:

WEB ADDRESS:

USERNAME:

PASSWORD:

NOTES:

e

WEB NAME:

WEB ADDRESS:

USERNAME:

PASSWORD:

NOTES:

WEB NAME:

WEB ADDRESS:

USERNAME:

PASSWORD:

NOTES:

WEB NAME: _____

WEB ADDRESS: _____

USERNAME: _____

PASSWORD: _____

NOTES: _____

_____

WEB NAME: _____

WEB ADDRESS: _____

USERNAME: _____

PASSWORD: _____

NOTES: _____

_____

WEB NAME: _____

WEB ADDRESS: _____

USERNAME: _____

PASSWORD: _____

NOTES: _____

_____

_____

WEB NAME:

WEB ADDRESS:

USERNAME:

PASSWORD:

NOTES:

WEB NAME:

WEB ADDRESS:

USERNAME:

PASSWORD:

NOTES:

WEB NAME:

WEB ADDRESS:

USERNAME:

PASSWORD:

NOTES:

WEB NAME: _____

WEB ADDRESS: _____

USERNAME: _____

PASSWORD: _____

NOTES: _____

_____

WEB NAME: _____

WEB ADDRESS: _____

USERNAME: _____

PASSWORD: _____

NOTES: _____

_____

WEB NAME: _____

WEB ADDRESS: _____

USERNAME: _____

PASSWORD: _____

NOTES: _____

WEB NAME: _____

WEB ADDRESS: _____

USERNAME: _____

PASSWORD: _____

NOTES: _____

_____

WEB NAME: _____

WEB ADDRESS: _____

USERNAME: _____

PASSWORD: _____

NOTES: _____

_____

WEB NAME: _____

WEB ADDRESS: _____

USERNAME: _____

PASSWORD: _____

NOTES: _____

_____

_____

WEB NAME: _____

WEB ADDRESS: _____

USERNAME: _____

PASSWORD: _____

NOTES: _____

_____

WEB NAME: _____

WEB ADDRESS: _____

USERNAME: _____

PASSWORD: _____

NOTES: _____

_____

_____

WEB NAME: _____

WEB ADDRESS: _____

USERNAME: _____

PASSWORD: _____

NOTES: _____

_____

_____

WEB NAME:

WEB ADDRESS:

USERNAME:

PASSWORD:

NOTES:

WEB NAME:

WEB ADDRESS:

USERNAME:

PASSWORD:

NOTES:

WEB NAME:

WEB ADDRESS:

USERNAME:

PASSWORD:

NOTES:

WEB NAME:

WEB ADDRESS:

USERNAME:

PASSWORD:

NOTES:

WEB NAME:

WEB ADDRESS:

USERNAME:

PASSWORD:

NOTES:

WEB NAME:

WEB ADDRESS:

USERNAME:

PASSWORD:

NOTES:

WEB NAME:

WEB ADDRESS:

USERNAME:

PASSWORD:

NOTES:

WEB NAME:

WEB ADDRESS:

USERNAME:

PASSWORD:

NOTES:

WEB NAME:

WEB ADDRESS:

USERNAME:

PASSWORD:

NOTES:

WEB NAME: _____

WEB ADDRESS: _____

USERNAME: _____

PASSWORD: _____

NOTES: _____

_____

G **WEB NAME:** _____

WEB ADDRESS: _____

USERNAME: _____

PASSWORD: _____

NOTES: _____

_____

WEB NAME: _____

WEB ADDRESS: _____

USERNAME: _____

PASSWORD: _____

NOTES: _____

_____

_____

WEB NAME: _____

WEB ADDRESS: _____

USERNAME: _____

PASSWORD: _____

NOTES: _____

_____

WEB NAME: _____

WEB ADDRESS: _____

USERNAME: _____

PASSWORD: _____

NOTES: _____

_____

WEB NAME: _____

WEB ADDRESS: _____

USERNAME: _____

PASSWORD: _____

NOTES: _____

_____

_____

WEB NAME: _____

WEB ADDRESS: _____

USERNAME: _____

PASSWORD: _____

NOTES: _____

_____

_____

G **WEB NAME:** _____

WEB ADDRESS: _____

USERNAME: _____

PASSWORD: _____

NOTES: _____

_____

_____

WEB NAME: _____

WEB ADDRESS: _____

USERNAME: _____

PASSWORD: _____

NOTES: _____

_____

_____

WEB NAME:

WEB ADDRESS:

USERNAME:

PASSWORD:

NOTES:

WEB NAME:

WEB ADDRESS:

USERNAME:

PASSWORD:

NOTES:

WEB NAME:

WEB ADDRESS:

USERNAME:

PASSWORD:

NOTES:

WEB NAME: _____

WEB ADDRESS: _____

USERNAME: _____

PASSWORD: _____

NOTES: _____

_____

_____

WEB NAME: _____

WEB ADDRESS: _____

USERNAME: _____

PASSWORD: _____

NOTES: _____

_____

_____

WEB NAME: _____

WEB ADDRESS: _____

USERNAME: _____

PASSWORD: _____

NOTES: _____

_____

_____

WEB NAME:

WEB ADDRESS:

USERNAME:

PASSWORD:

NOTES:

WEB NAME:

WEB ADDRESS:

USERNAME:

PASSWORD:

NOTES:

WEB NAME:

WEB ADDRESS:

USERNAME:

PASSWORD:

NOTES:

WEB NAME: _____

WEB ADDRESS: _____

USERNAME: _____

PASSWORD: _____

NOTES: _____

_____

_____

WEB NAME: _____

WEB ADDRESS: _____

USERNAME: _____

PASSWORD: _____

NOTES: _____

_____

_____

WEB NAME: _____

WEB ADDRESS: _____

USERNAME: _____

PASSWORD: _____

NOTES: _____

_____

_____

WEB NAME:

WEB ADDRESS:

USERNAME:

PASSWORD:

NOTES:

WEB NAME:

WEB ADDRESS:

USERNAME:

PASSWORD:

NOTES:

WEB NAME:

WEB ADDRESS:

USERNAME:

PASSWORD:

NOTES:

WEB NAME: _____

WEB ADDRESS: _____

USERNAME: _____

PASSWORD: _____

NOTES: _____

_____

_____

WEB NAME: _____

WEB ADDRESS: _____

USERNAME: _____

PASSWORD: _____

NOTES: _____

_____

_____

WEB NAME: _____

WEB ADDRESS: _____

USERNAME: _____

PASSWORD: _____

NOTES: _____

_____

_____

WEB NAME:

WEB ADDRESS:

USERNAME:

PASSWORD:

NOTES:

WEB NAME:

WEB ADDRESS:

USERNAME:

PASSWORD:

NOTES:

WEB NAME:

WEB ADDRESS:

USERNAME:

PASSWORD:

NOTES:

WEB NAME: _____

WEB ADDRESS: _____

USERNAME: _____

PASSWORD: _____

NOTES: _____

_____

_____

WEB NAME: _____

WEB ADDRESS: _____

USERNAME: _____

PASSWORD: _____

NOTES: _____

_____

_____

WEB NAME: _____

WEB ADDRESS: _____

USERNAME: _____

PASSWORD: _____

NOTES: _____

_____

_____

WEB NAME: _____

WEB ADDRESS: _____

USERNAME: _____

PASSWORD: _____

NOTES: _____

_____

_____

WEB NAME: _____

WEB ADDRESS: _____

USERNAME: _____

PASSWORD: _____

NOTES: _____

_____

_____

WEB NAME: _____

WEB ADDRESS: _____

USERNAME: _____

PASSWORD: _____

NOTES: _____

_____

_____

WEB NAME:

WEB ADDRESS:

USERNAME:

PASSWORD:

NOTES:

WEB NAME:

WEB ADDRESS:

J **USERNAME:**

PASSWORD:

NOTES:

WEB NAME:

WEB ADDRESS:

USERNAME:

PASSWORD:

NOTES:

WEB NAME:

WEB ADDRESS:

USERNAME:

PASSWORD:

NOTES:

WEB NAME:

WEB ADDRESS:

USERNAME:

J

PASSWORD:

NOTES:

WEB NAME:

WEB ADDRESS:

USERNAME:

PASSWORD:

NOTES:

WEB NAME:

WEB ADDRESS:

USERNAME:

PASSWORD:

NOTES:

WEB NAME:

WEB ADDRESS:

USERNAME:

PASSWORD:

NOTES:

WEB NAME:

WEB ADDRESS:

USERNAME:

PASSWORD:

NOTES:

WEB NAME:

WEB ADDRESS:

USERNAME:

PASSWORD:

NOTES:

WEB NAME:

WEB ADDRESS:

USERNAME: *J*

PASSWORD:

NOTES:

WEB NAME:

WEB ADDRESS:

USERNAME:

PASSWORD:

NOTES:

WEB NAME:

WEB ADDRESS:

USERNAME:

PASSWORD:

NOTES:

WEB NAME:

WEB ADDRESS:

J **USERNAME:**

PASSWORD:

NOTES:

WEB NAME:

WEB ADDRESS:

USERNAME:

PASSWORD:

NOTES:

WEB NAME:

WEB ADDRESS:

USERNAME:

PASSWORD:

NOTES:

WEB NAME:

WEB ADDRESS:

USERNAME:

J

PASSWORD:

NOTES:

WEB NAME:

WEB ADDRESS:

USERNAME:

PASSWORD:

NOTES:

WEB NAME:

WEB ADDRESS:

USERNAME:

PASSWORD:

NOTES:

WEB NAME:

WEB ADDRESS:

USERNAME:

PASSWORD:

NOTES:

WEB NAME:

WEB ADDRESS:

USERNAME:

PASSWORD:

NOTES:

WEB NAME: _____

WEB ADDRESS: _____

USERNAME: _____

PASSWORD: _____

NOTES: _____

_____

WEB NAME: _____

WEB ADDRESS: _____

USERNAME: _____

PASSWORD: _____

NOTES: _____

_____

WEB NAME: _____

WEB ADDRESS: _____

USERNAME: _____

PASSWORD: _____

NOTES: _____

_____

_____

WEB NAME:

WEB ADDRESS:

USERNAME:

PASSWORD:

NOTES:

WEB NAME:

WEB ADDRESS:

USERNAME:

J **PASSWORD:**

NOTES:

WEB NAME:

WEB ADDRESS:

USERNAME:

PASSWORD:

NOTES:

WEB NAME:

WEB ADDRESS:

USERNAME:

PASSWORD:

NOTES:

WEB NAME:

WEB ADDRESS:

USERNAME:

PASSWORD:

NOTES:

WEB NAME:

WEB ADDRESS:

USERNAME:

PASSWORD:

NOTES:

WEB NAME:

WEB ADDRESS:

USERNAME:

PASSWORD:

NOTES:

WEB NAME:

WEB ADDRESS:

USERNAME:

PASSWORD:

NOTES:

WEB NAME:

WEB ADDRESS:

USERNAME:

PASSWORD:

NOTES:

WEB NAME:

WEB ADDRESS:

USERNAME:

PASSWORD:

NOTES:

WEB NAME:

WEB ADDRESS:

USERNAME:

PASSWORD:

J

NOTES:

WEB NAME:

WEB ADDRESS:

USERNAME:

PASSWORD:

NOTES:

WEB NAME: _____

WEB ADDRESS: _____

USERNAME: _____

PASSWORD: _____

NOTES: _____

_____

_____

WEB NAME: _____

WEB ADDRESS: _____

USERNAME: _____

PASSWORD: _____

NOTES: _____

_____

_____

WEB NAME: _____

WEB ADDRESS: _____

USERNAME: _____

PASSWORD: _____

NOTES: _____

_____

_____

WEB NAME: _____

WEB ADDRESS: _____

USERNAME: _____

PASSWORD: _____

NOTES: _____

_____

_____

WEB NAME: _____

WEB ADDRESS: _____

USERNAME: _____

PASSWORD: _____

NOTES: _____

_____

_____

WEB NAME: _____

WEB ADDRESS: _____

USERNAME: _____

PASSWORD: _____

NOTES: _____

_____

_____

WEB NAME: _____

WEB ADDRESS: _____

USERNAME: _____

PASSWORD: _____

NOTES: _____

_____

_____

WEB NAME: _____

WEB ADDRESS: _____

USERNAME: _____

PASSWORD: _____

NOTES: _____

_____

_____

WEB NAME: _____

WEB ADDRESS: _____

USERNAME: _____

PASSWORD: _____

NOTES: _____

_____

_____

WEB NAME:

WEB ADDRESS:

USERNAME:

PASSWORD:

NOTES:

WEB NAME:

WEB ADDRESS:

USERNAME:

PASSWORD:

NOTES:

WEB NAME:

WEB ADDRESS:

USERNAME:

PASSWORD:

NOTES:

WEB NAME: _____

WEB ADDRESS: _____

USERNAME: _____

PASSWORD: _____

NOTES: _____

_____

_____

WEB NAME: _____

WEB ADDRESS: _____

USERNAME: _____

PASSWORD: _____

NOTES: _____

_____

_____

WEB NAME: _____

WEB ADDRESS: _____

USERNAME: _____

PASSWORD: _____

NOTES: _____

_____

_____

WEB NAME:

WEB ADDRESS:

USERNAME:

PASSWORD:

NOTES:

WEB NAME:

WEB ADDRESS:

USERNAME:

PASSWORD:

NOTES:

WEB NAME:

WEB ADDRESS:

USERNAME:

PASSWORD:

NOTES:

WEB NAME:

WEB ADDRESS:

USERNAME:

PASSWORD:

NOTES:

WEB NAME:

WEB ADDRESS:

USERNAME:

PASSWORD:

NOTES:

WEB NAME:

WEB ADDRESS:

USERNAME:

PASSWORD:

NOTES:

WEB NAME:

WEB ADDRESS:

USERNAME:

PASSWORD:

NOTES:

WEB NAME:

WEB ADDRESS:

USERNAME:

PASSWORD:

NOTES:

WEB NAME:

WEB ADDRESS:

USERNAME:

PASSWORD:

NOTES:

WEB NAME:

WEB ADDRESS:

USERNAME:

PASSWORD:

NOTES:

WEB NAME:

WEB ADDRESS:

USERNAME:

PASSWORD:

NOTES:

WEB NAME:

WEB ADDRESS:

USERNAME:

PASSWORD:

NOTES:

WEB NAME:

WEB ADDRESS:

USERNAME:

PASSWORD:

NOTES:

WEB NAME:

WEB ADDRESS:

USERNAME:

PASSWORD:

NOTES:

WEB NAME:

WEB ADDRESS:

USERNAME:

PASSWORD:

NOTES:

WEB NAME:

WEB ADDRESS:

USERNAME:

PASSWORD:

NOTES:

WEB NAME:

WEB ADDRESS:

USERNAME:

PASSWORD:

NOTES:

WEB NAME:

WEB ADDRESS:

USERNAME:

PASSWORD:

NOTES:

WEB NAME:

WEB ADDRESS:

USERNAME:

PASSWORD:

NOTES:

WEB NAME:

WEB ADDRESS:

USERNAME:

PASSWORD:

NOTES:

L

WEB NAME:

WEB ADDRESS:

USERNAME:

PASSWORD:

NOTES:

WEB NAME:

WEB ADDRESS:

USERNAME:

PASSWORD:

NOTES:

WEB NAME:

WEB ADDRESS:

USERNAME:

PASSWORD:

NOTES:

WEB NAME:

WEB ADDRESS:

USERNAME:

PASSWORD:

NOTES:

WEB NAME:

WEB ADDRESS:

USERNAME:

PASSWORD:

NOTES:

WEB NAME:

WEB ADDRESS:

USERNAME:

PASSWORD:

NOTES:

M

WEB NAME:

WEB ADDRESS:

USERNAME:

PASSWORD:

NOTES:

WEB NAME:

WEB ADDRESS:

USERNAME:

PASSWORD:

NOTES:

WEB NAME:

WEB ADDRESS:

USERNAME:

PASSWORD:

NOTES:

WEB NAME:

WEB ADDRESS:

USERNAME:

PASSWORD:

NOTES:

WEB NAME:

WEB ADDRESS:

USERNAME:

PASSWORD:

NOTES:

WEB NAME:

WEB ADDRESS:

USERNAME:

PASSWORD:

NOTES:

WEB NAME:

WEB ADDRESS:

USERNAME:

PASSWORD:

NOTES:

WEB NAME:

WEB ADDRESS:

USERNAME:

PASSWORD:

NOTES:

WEB NAME:

WEB ADDRESS:

USERNAME:

PASSWORD:

NOTES:

WEB NAME:

WEB ADDRESS:

USERNAME:

PASSWORD:

NOTES:

WEB NAME:

WEB ADDRESS:

USERNAME:

PASSWORD:

NOTES:

WEB NAME:

WEB ADDRESS:

USERNAME:

PASSWORD:

NOTES:

M

WEB NAME:

WEB ADDRESS:

USERNAME:

PASSWORD:

NOTES:

WEB NAME:

WEB ADDRESS:

USERNAME:

PASSWORD:

NOTES:

WEB NAME:

WEB ADDRESS:

USERNAME:

PASSWORD:

NOTES:

N **WEB NAME:**

WEB ADDRESS:

USERNAME:

PASSWORD:

NOTES:

WEB NAME:

WEB ADDRESS:

USERNAME:

PASSWORD:

NOTES:

WEB NAME:

WEB ADDRESS:

USERNAME:

PASSWORD:

NOTES:

WEB NAME:

WEB ADDRESS:

USERNAME:

PASSWORD:

NOTES:

WEB NAME: _____

WEB ADDRESS: _____

USERNAME: _____

PASSWORD: _____

NOTES: _____

_____

_____

WEB NAME: _____

WEB ADDRESS: _____

USERNAME: _____

PASSWORD: _____

NOTES: _____

_____

_____

WEB NAME: _____

WEB ADDRESS: _____

USERNAME: _____

PASSWORD: _____

NOTES: _____

_____

_____

WEB NAME: _____

WEB ADDRESS: _____

USERNAME: _____

PASSWORD: _____

NOTES: _____

_____

_____

WEB NAME: _____

WEB ADDRESS: _____

USERNAME: _____

PASSWORD: _____

NOTES: _____

_____

_____

WEB NAME: _____

WEB ADDRESS: _____

USERNAME: _____

PASSWORD: _____

NOTES: _____

_____

_____

WEB NAME:

WEB ADDRESS:

USERNAME:

PASSWORD:

NOTES:

WEB NAME:

WEB ADDRESS:

USERNAME:

PASSWORD:

NOTES:

WEB NAME:

WEB ADDRESS:

USERNAME:

PASSWORD:

NOTES:

WEB NAME:

WEB ADDRESS:

USERNAME:

PASSWORD:

NOTES:

WEB NAME:

WEB ADDRESS:

USERNAME:

PASSWORD:

NOTES:

WEB NAME:

WEB ADDRESS:

USERNAME:

PASSWORD:

NOTES:

WEB NAME:

WEB ADDRESS:

USERNAME:

PASSWORD:

NOTES:

WEB NAME:

WEB ADDRESS:

USERNAME:

PASSWORD:

NOTES:

WEB NAME:

WEB ADDRESS:

USERNAME:

PASSWORD:

NOTES:

WEB NAME:

WEB ADDRESS:

USERNAME:

PASSWORD:

NOTES:

WEB NAME:

WEB ADDRESS:

USERNAME:

PASSWORD:

NOTES:

WEB NAME:

WEB ADDRESS:

USERNAME:

PASSWORD:

NOTES:

WEB NAME:

WEB ADDRESS:

USERNAME:

PASSWORD:

NOTES:

WEB NAME:

WEB ADDRESS:

USERNAME:

PASSWORD:

NOTES:

WEB NAME:

WEB ADDRESS:

USERNAME:

PASSWORD:

NOTES:

WEB NAME:

WEB ADDRESS:

USERNAME:

PASSWORD:

NOTES:

WEB NAME:

WEB ADDRESS:

USERNAME:

PASSWORD:

NOTES:

WEB NAME:

WEB ADDRESS:

USERNAME:

PASSWORD:

NOTES:

WEB NAME: _____

WEB ADDRESS: _____

USERNAME: _____

PASSWORD: _____

NOTES: _____

_____

_____

WEB NAME: _____

WEB ADDRESS: _____

USERNAME: _____

PASSWORD: _____

NOTES: _____

_____

_____

WEB NAME: _____

WEB ADDRESS: _____

USERNAME: _____

PASSWORD: _____

NOTES: _____

_____

_____

WEB NAME:

WEB ADDRESS:

USERNAME:

PASSWORD:

NOTES:

WEB NAME:

WEB ADDRESS:

USERNAME:

PASSWORD:

NOTES:

WEB NAME:

WEB ADDRESS:

USERNAME:

PASSWORD:

NOTES:

WEB NAME: _____

WEB ADDRESS: _____

USERNAME: _____

PASSWORD: _____

NOTES: _____

_____

_____

WEB NAME: _____

WEB ADDRESS: _____

USERNAME: _____

PASSWORD: _____

NOTES: _____

_____

_____

WEB NAME: _____

WEB ADDRESS: _____

USERNAME: _____

PASSWORD: _____

NOTES: _____

_____

_____

WEB NAME:

WEB ADDRESS:

USERNAME:

PASSWORD:

NOTES:

WEB NAME:

WEB ADDRESS:

USERNAME:

PASSWORD:

NOTES:

WEB NAME:

WEB ADDRESS:

USERNAME:

PASSWORD:

NOTES:

WEB NAME: _____

WEB ADDRESS: _____

USERNAME: _____

PASSWORD: _____

NOTES: _____

_____

_____

WEB NAME: _____

WEB ADDRESS: _____

USERNAME: _____

PASSWORD: _____

NOTES: _____

_____

_____

WEB NAME: _____

WEB ADDRESS: _____

USERNAME: _____

PASSWORD: _____

NOTES: _____

_____

_____

WEB NAME:

WEB ADDRESS:

USERNAME:

PASSWORD:

NOTES:

WEB NAME:

WEB ADDRESS:

USERNAME:

PASSWORD:

NOTES:

WEB NAME:

WEB ADDRESS:

USERNAME:

PASSWORD:

NOTES:

WEB NAME:

WEB ADDRESS:

USERNAME:

PASSWORD:

NOTES:

WEB NAME:

WEB ADDRESS:

USERNAME:

PASSWORD:

NOTES:

WEB NAME:

WEB ADDRESS:

USERNAME:

PASSWORD:

NOTES:

WEB NAME:

WEB ADDRESS:

USERNAME:

PASSWORD:

NOTES:

WEB NAME:

WEB ADDRESS:

USERNAME:

PASSWORD:

NOTES:

WEB NAME:

WEB ADDRESS:

USERNAME:

PASSWORD:

NOTES:

WEB NAME:

WEB ADDRESS:

USERNAME:

PASSWORD:

NOTES:

WEB NAME:

WEB ADDRESS:

USERNAME:

PASSWORD:

NOTES:

WEB NAME:

WEB ADDRESS:

USERNAME:

PASSWORD:

NOTES:

WEB NAME: _____

WEB ADDRESS: _____

USERNAME: _____

PASSWORD: _____

NOTES: _____

_____

WEB NAME: _____

WEB ADDRESS: _____

USERNAME: _____

PASSWORD: _____

NOTES: _____

_____

WEB NAME: _____

WEB ADDRESS: _____

USERNAME: _____

PASSWORD: _____

NOTES: _____

_____

_____

WEB NAME:

WEB ADDRESS:

USERNAME:

PASSWORD:

NOTES:

WEB NAME:

WEB ADDRESS:

USERNAME:

PASSWORD:

NOTES:

WEB NAME:

WEB ADDRESS:

USERNAME:

PASSWORD:

NOTES:

WEB NAME:

WEB ADDRESS:

USERNAME:

PASSWORD:

NOTES:

WEB NAME:

WEB ADDRESS:

USERNAME:

PASSWORD:

NOTES:

WEB NAME:

WEB ADDRESS:

USERNAME:

PASSWORD:

NOTES:

WEB NAME:

WEB ADDRESS:

USERNAME:

PASSWORD:

NOTES:

WEB NAME:

WEB ADDRESS:

USERNAME:

PASSWORD:

NOTES:

WEB NAME:

WEB ADDRESS:

USERNAME:

Q **PASSWORD:**

NOTES:

WEB NAME:

WEB ADDRESS:

USERNAME:

PASSWORD:

NOTES:

WEB NAME:

WEB ADDRESS:

USERNAME:

PASSWORD:

NOTES:

WEB NAME:

WEB ADDRESS:

USERNAME:

PASSWORD:

NOTES:

WEB NAME:

WEB ADDRESS:

USERNAME:

PASSWORD:

NOTES:

WEB NAME:

WEB ADDRESS:

USERNAME:

PASSWORD:

NOTES:

WEB NAME:

WEB ADDRESS:

USERNAME:

PASSWORD:

NOTES:

WEB NAME:

WEB ADDRESS:

USERNAME:

PASSWORD:

NOTES:

WEB NAME:

WEB ADDRESS:

USERNAME:

PASSWORD:

NOTES:

WEB NAME:

WEB ADDRESS:

USERNAME:

PASSWORD:

NOTES:

WEB NAME:

WEB ADDRESS:

USERNAME:

PASSWORD:

NOTES:

WEB NAME:

WEB ADDRESS:

USERNAME:

PASSWORD:

NOTES:

WEB NAME:

WEB ADDRESS:

USERNAME:

PASSWORD:

NOTES:

WEB NAME:

WEB ADDRESS:

USERNAME:

PASSWORD:

NOTES:

WEB NAME:

WEB ADDRESS:

USERNAME:

PASSWORD:

NOTES:

WEB NAME:

WEB ADDRESS:

USERNAME:

PASSWORD:

NOTES:

WEB NAME:

WEB ADDRESS:

USERNAME:

PASSWORD:

NOTES:

WEB NAME:

WEB ADDRESS:

USERNAME:

PASSWORD:

NOTES:

WEB NAME:

WEB ADDRESS:

USERNAME:

PASSWORD:

NOTES:

WEB NAME:

WEB ADDRESS:

USERNAME:

PASSWORD:

NOTES:

WEB NAME:

WEB ADDRESS:

USERNAME:

PASSWORD:

NOTES:

WEB NAME:

WEB ADDRESS:

USERNAME:

PASSWORD:

NOTES:

WEB NAME:

WEB ADDRESS:

USERNAME:

PASSWORD:

NOTES:

WEB NAME:

WEB ADDRESS:

USERNAME:

PASSWORD:

NOTES:

WEB NAME:

WEB ADDRESS:

USERNAME:

PASSWORD:

NOTES:

WEB NAME:

WEB ADDRESS:

USERNAME:

PASSWORD:

NOTES:

WEB NAME:

WEB ADDRESS:

USERNAME:

PASSWORD:

NOTES:

WEB NAME:

WEB ADDRESS:

USERNAME:

PASSWORD:

NOTES:

WEB NAME:

WEB ADDRESS:

USERNAME:

PASSWORD:

NOTES:

WEB NAME:

WEB ADDRESS:

USERNAME:

PASSWORD:

NOTES:

WEB NAME:

WEB ADDRESS:

USERNAME:

PASSWORD:

NOTES:

WEB NAME:

WEB ADDRESS:

USERNAME:

PASSWORD:

NOTES:

WEB NAME:

WEB ADDRESS:

USERNAME:

PASSWORD:

NOTES:

WEB NAME:

WEB ADDRESS:

USERNAME:

PASSWORD:

NOTES:

WEB NAME:

WEB ADDRESS:

USERNAME:

PASSWORD:

NOTES:

WEB NAME:

WEB ADDRESS:

USERNAME:

PASSWORD:

NOTES:

WEB NAME:

S **WEB ADDRESS:**

USERNAME:

PASSWORD:

NOTES:

WEB NAME:

WEB ADDRESS:

USERNAME:

PASSWORD:

NOTES:

WEB NAME:

WEB ADDRESS:

USERNAME:

PASSWORD:

NOTES:

WEB NAME:

WEB ADDRESS:

USERNAME:

PASSWORD:

NOTES:

WEB NAME: _____

WEB ADDRESS: _____

USERNAME: _____

PASSWORD: _____

NOTES: _____

_____

_____

WEB NAME: _____

WEB ADDRESS: _____

USERNAME: _____

PASSWORD: _____

NOTES: _____

_____

_____

WEB NAME: _____

WEB ADDRESS: _____

USERNAME: _____

PASSWORD: _____

NOTES: _____

_____

_____

WEB NAME:

WEB ADDRESS:

USERNAME:

PASSWORD:

NOTES:

WEB NAME:

WEB ADDRESS:

USERNAME:

PASSWORD:

NOTES:

WEB NAME:

WEB ADDRESS:

USERNAME:

PASSWORD:

NOTES:

WEB NAME:

WEB ADDRESS:

USERNAME:

PASSWORD:

NOTES:

WEB NAME:

WEB ADDRESS:

USERNAME:

PASSWORD:

NOTES:

WEB NAME:

WEB ADDRESS:

USERNAME:

PASSWORD:

NOTES:

WEB NAME:

WEB ADDRESS:

USERNAME:

PASSWORD:

NOTES:

WEB NAME:

WEB ADDRESS:

USERNAME:

PASSWORD:

NOTES:

WEB NAME:

WEB ADDRESS:

USERNAME:

PASSWORD:

NOTES:

WEB NAME:

WEB ADDRESS:

USERNAME:

PASSWORD:

NOTES:

WEB NAME:

WEB ADDRESS:

USERNAME:

PASSWORD:

NOTES:

WEB NAME:

WEB ADDRESS:

USERNAME:

PASSWORD:

NOTES:

WEB NAME:

WEB ADDRESS:

USERNAME:

PASSWORD:

NOTES:

WEB NAME:

WEB ADDRESS:

USERNAME:

PASSWORD:

NOTES:

WEB NAME:

WEB ADDRESS:

USERNAME:

PASSWORD:

NOTES:

WEB NAME: _____

WEB ADDRESS: _____

USERNAME: _____

PASSWORD: _____

NOTES: _____

_____

_____

WEB NAME: _____

WEB ADDRESS: _____

USERNAME: _____

PASSWORD: _____

NOTES: _____

_____

_____

WEB NAME: _____

WEB ADDRESS: _____

USERNAME: _____

PASSWORD: _____

NOTES: _____

_____

_____

WEB NAME:

WEB ADDRESS:

USERNAME:

PASSWORD:

NOTES:

WEB NAME:

WEB ADDRESS:

USERNAME:

PASSWORD:

NOTES:

WEB NAME:

WEB ADDRESS:

USERNAME:

PASSWORD:

NOTES:

WEB NAME:

WEB ADDRESS:

USERNAME:

PASSWORD:

NOTES:

WEB NAME:

WEB ADDRESS:

USERNAME:

PASSWORD:

NOTES:

WEB NAME:

WEB ADDRESS:

USERNAME:

u **PASSWORD:**

NOTES:

WEB NAME:

WEB ADDRESS:

USERNAME:

PASSWORD:

NOTES:

WEB NAME:

WEB ADDRESS:

USERNAME:

PASSWORD:

NOTES:

WEB NAME:

WEB ADDRESS:

USERNAME:

PASSWORD:

NOTES:

WEB NAME:

WEB ADDRESS:

USERNAME:

PASSWORD:

NOTES:

WEB NAME:

WEB ADDRESS:

USERNAME:

PASSWORD:

NOTES:

WEB NAME:

WEB ADDRESS:

USERNAME:

u **PASSWORD:**

NOTES:

WEB NAME:

WEB ADDRESS:

USERNAME:

PASSWORD:

NOTES:

WEB NAME:

WEB ADDRESS:

USERNAME:

PASSWORD:

NOTES:

WEB NAME:

WEB ADDRESS:

USERNAME:

PASSWORD:

NOTES:

u

WEB NAME: _____

WEB ADDRESS: _____

USERNAME: _____

PASSWORD: _____

NOTES: _____

_____

WEB NAME: _____

WEB ADDRESS: _____

USERNAME: _____

PASSWORD: _____

NOTES: _____

_____

WEB NAME: _____

WEB ADDRESS: _____

USERNAME: _____

PASSWORD: _____

NOTES: _____

_____

_____

WEB NAME:

WEB ADDRESS:

USERNAME:

PASSWORD:

NOTES:

WEB NAME:

WEB ADDRESS:

USERNAME:

PASSWORD:

NOTES:

WEB NAME:

WEB ADDRESS:

USERNAME:

PASSWORD:

NOTES:

WEB NAME:

WEB ADDRESS:

USERNAME:

PASSWORD:

NOTES:

WEB NAME:

WEB ADDRESS:

USERNAME:

PASSWORD:

NOTES:

WEB NAME:

WEB ADDRESS:

USERNAME:

PASSWORD:

NOTES:

WEB NAME:

WEB ADDRESS:

USERNAME:

PASSWORD:

NOTES:

WEB NAME:

WEB ADDRESS:

USERNAME:

PASSWORD:

NOTES:

WEB NAME:

WEB ADDRESS:

USERNAME:

PASSWORD:

NOTES:

WEB NAME: _____

WEB ADDRESS: _____

USERNAME: _____

PASSWORD: _____

NOTES: _____

_____

WEB NAME: _____

WEB ADDRESS: _____

USERNAME: _____

PASSWORD: _____

NOTES: _____

_____

WEB NAME: _____

WEB ADDRESS: _____

USERNAME: _____

PASSWORD: _____

NOTES: _____

_____

_____

WEB NAME:

WEB ADDRESS:

USERNAME:

PASSWORD:

NOTES:

WEB NAME:

WEB ADDRESS:

USERNAME:

PASSWORD:

NOTES:

WEB NAME:

WEB ADDRESS:

USERNAME:

PASSWORD:

NOTES:

WEB NAME:

WEB ADDRESS:

USERNAME:

PASSWORD:

NOTES:

WEB NAME:

WEB ADDRESS:

USERNAME:

PASSWORD:

NOTES:

WEB NAME:

WEB ADDRESS:

USERNAME:

PASSWORD:

NOTES:

WEB NAME:

WEB ADDRESS:

USERNAME:

PASSWORD:

NOTES:

WEB NAME:

WEB ADDRESS:

USERNAME:

PASSWORD:

NOTES:

WEB NAME:

WEB ADDRESS:

USERNAME:

PASSWORD:

NOTES:

V

WEB NAME:

WEB ADDRESS:

USERNAME:

PASSWORD:

NOTES:

WEB NAME:

WEB ADDRESS:

USERNAME:

PASSWORD:

NOTES:

WEB NAME:

WEB ADDRESS:

USERNAME:

PASSWORD:

NOTES:

WEB NAME:

WEB ADDRESS:

USERNAME:

PASSWORD:

NOTES:

WEB NAME:

WEB ADDRESS:

USERNAME:

PASSWORD:

NOTES:

WEB NAME:

WEB ADDRESS:

USERNAME:

PASSWORD:

NOTES:

WEB NAME:

WEB ADDRESS:

USERNAME:

PASSWORD:

NOTES:

WEB NAME:

WEB ADDRESS:

USERNAME:

PASSWORD:

NOTES:

WEB NAME:

WEB ADDRESS:

USERNAME:

PASSWORD:

NOTES:

WEB NAME:

WEB ADDRESS:

USERNAME:

PASSWORD:

NOTES:

WEB NAME:

WEB ADDRESS:

USERNAME:

PASSWORD:

NOTES:

WEB NAME:

WEB ADDRESS:

USERNAME:

PASSWORD:

NOTES:

WEB NAME:

WEB ADDRESS:

USERNAME:

PASSWORD:

NOTES:

WEB NAME:

WEB ADDRESS:

USERNAME:

PASSWORD:

NOTES:

WEB NAME:

WEB ADDRESS:

USERNAME:

PASSWORD:

NOTES:

WEB NAME: _____

WEB ADDRESS: _____

USERNAME: _____

PASSWORD: _____

NOTES: _____

_____

_____

WEB NAME: _____

WEB ADDRESS: _____

USERNAME: _____

PASSWORD: _____

NOTES: _____

_____

_____

WEB NAME: _____

WEB ADDRESS: _____

USERNAME: _____

PASSWORD: _____

NOTES: _____

_____

_____

WEB NAME:

WEB ADDRESS:

USERNAME:

PASSWORD:

NOTES:

WEB NAME:

WEB ADDRESS:

USERNAME:

PASSWORD:

NOTES:

WEB NAME:

WEB ADDRESS:

USERNAME:

PASSWORD:

NOTES:

X

WEB NAME:

WEB ADDRESS:

USERNAME:

PASSWORD:

NOTES:

WEB NAME:

WEB ADDRESS:

USERNAME:

PASSWORD:

NOTES:

WEB NAME:

WEB ADDRESS:

USERNAME:

PASSWORD:

NOTES:

X

WEB NAME:

WEB ADDRESS:

USERNAME:

PASSWORD:

NOTES:

WEB NAME:

WEB ADDRESS:

USERNAME:

PASSWORD:

NOTES:

WEB NAME:

WEB ADDRESS:

USERNAME:

PASSWORD:

NOTES:

X

WEB NAME:

WEB ADDRESS:

USERNAME:

PASSWORD:

NOTES:

WEB NAME:

WEB ADDRESS:

USERNAME:

PASSWORD:

NOTES:

WEB NAME:

WEB ADDRESS:

USERNAME:

PASSWORD:

NOTES:

X

WEB NAME: _____

WEB ADDRESS: _____

USERNAME: _____

PASSWORD: _____

NOTES: _____

_____

_____

WEB NAME: _____

WEB ADDRESS: _____

USERNAME: _____

PASSWORD: _____

NOTES: _____

_____

_____

WEB NAME: _____

WEB ADDRESS: _____

USERNAME: _____

PASSWORD: _____

NOTES: _____

X _____

_____

WEB NAME:

WEB ADDRESS:

USERNAME:

PASSWORD:

NOTES:

WEB NAME:

WEB ADDRESS:

USERNAME:

PASSWORD:

NOTES:

WEB NAME:

WEB ADDRESS:

USERNAME:

PASSWORD:

NOTES:

X

y

WEB NAME:

WEB ADDRESS:

USERNAME:

PASSWORD:

NOTES:

WEB NAME:

WEB ADDRESS:

USERNAME:

PASSWORD:

NOTES:

WEB NAME:

WEB ADDRESS:

USERNAME:

PASSWORD:

NOTES:

WEB NAME:

WEB ADDRESS:

USERNAME:

PASSWORD:

NOTES:

WEB NAME:

WEB ADDRESS:

USERNAME:

PASSWORD:

NOTES:

WEB NAME:

WEB ADDRESS:

USERNAME:

PASSWORD:

NOTES:

WEB NAME:

WEB ADDRESS:

USERNAME:

PASSWORD:

NOTES:

WEB NAME:

WEB ADDRESS:

USERNAME:

PASSWORD:

NOTES:

WEB NAME:

WEB ADDRESS:

USERNAME:

PASSWORD:

NOTES:

WEB NAME:

WEB ADDRESS:

USERNAME:

PASSWORD:

NOTES:

WEB NAME:

WEB ADDRESS:

USERNAME:

PASSWORD:

NOTES:

WEB NAME:

WEB ADDRESS:

USERNAME:

PASSWORD:

NOTES:

Y

WEB NAME:

WEB ADDRESS:

USERNAME:

PASSWORD:

NOTES:

WEB NAME:

WEB ADDRESS:

USERNAME:

PASSWORD:

NOTES:

WEB NAME:

WEB ADDRESS:

USERNAME:

PASSWORD:

NOTES:

WEB NAME:

WEB ADDRESS:

USERNAME:

PASSWORD:

NOTES:

WEB NAME:

WEB ADDRESS:

USERNAME:

PASSWORD:

NOTES:

WEB NAME:

WEB ADDRESS:

USERNAME:

PASSWORD:

NOTES:

WEB NAME:

WEB ADDRESS:

Z **USERNAME:**

PASSWORD:

NOTES:

WEB NAME:

WEB ADDRESS:

USERNAME:

PASSWORD:

NOTES:

WEB NAME:

WEB ADDRESS:

USERNAME:

PASSWORD:

NOTES:

WEB NAME:

WEB ADDRESS:

USERNAME:

PASSWORD:

NOTES:

WEB NAME:

WEB ADDRESS:

USERNAME:

PASSWORD:

NOTES:

WEB NAME:

WEB ADDRESS:

USERNAME:

PASSWORD:

NOTES:

WEB NAME:

WEB ADDRESS:

Z **USERNAME:**

PASSWORD:

NOTES:

WEB NAME:

WEB ADDRESS:

USERNAME:

PASSWORD:

NOTES:

WEB NAME:

WEB ADDRESS:

USERNAME:

PASSWORD:

NOTES:

WEB NAME:

WEB ADDRESS:

USERNAME:

PASSWORD:

NOTES:

WEB NAME:

WEB ADDRESS:

USERNAME:

PASSWORD:

NOTES:

WEB NAME:

WEB ADDRESS:

USERNAME:

PASSWORD:

NOTES:

WEB NAME:

WEB ADDRESS:

Z **USERNAME:**

PASSWORD:

NOTES:

WEB NAME:

WEB ADDRESS:

USERNAME:

PASSWORD:

NOTES:

WEB NAME:

WEB ADDRESS:

USERNAME:

PASSWORD:

NOTES:

WEB NAME:

WEB ADDRESS:

USERNAME:

PASSWORD:

NOTES:

WEB NAME:

WEB ADDRESS:

USERNAME:

PASSWORD:

NOTES:

WEB NAME:

WEB ADDRESS:

USERNAME:

PASSWORD:

NOTES:

NOTES:

NOTES:

NOTES:

NOTES:

NOTES:

NOTES:

NOTES:

NOTES:

NOTES:

NOTES:

NOTES:

NOTES:

www.ingramcontent.com/pod-product-compliance
Lightning Source LLC
Chambersburg PA
CBHW060851170526
45158CB00001B/308